ADVENTURERS IN HISTORY

TENZING NORGAY CLIMBS MOUNT EVEREST

by Janie Havemeyer
illustrated by Cesar Samaniego

Grasshopper Books, an imprint of Jump! Library by FlutterBee

Tools for Parents & Teachers

Grasshopper Books enhance imagination and introduce the earliest readers to fun storylines and illustrations. The easy-to-read text supports early reading experiences with repetitive sentence patterns and sight words.

Before Reading

- Discuss the cover illustration. What do readers see?
- Look at the glossary together. Discuss the words.

During Reading

- "Walk" through the book with the reader. Discuss new or unfamiliar words. Sound them out together.
- Look at the illustrations. When and where does the story take place? What is happening in the story?

After Reading

- Prompt the child to think more. Ask: Would you like to climb Mount Everest? Why or why not?

Grasshopper Books are published by Jump!
3500 American Blvd W, Suite 150
Bloomington, MN 55431
www.jumplibrary.com

Jump! is a division of FlutterBee Education Group.

Library of Congress Cataloging-in-Publication Data

Names: Havemeyer, Janie, author
Samaniego, César, 1975- illustrator
Title: Tenzing Norgay climbs Mount Everest / by Janie Havemeyer; illustrated Cesar Samaniego.
Description: Bloomington, MN: Jump!, Inc., [2026]
Series: Adventurers in history | Includes index.
Audience: Ages 7–10
Identifiers: LCCN 2025022984 (print)
LCCN 2025022985 (ebook)
ISBN 9798896621843 (hardcover)
ISBN 9798896621850 (paperback)
ISBN 9798896621867 (ebook)
Subjects: LCSH: Tenzing Norkey, 1914–1986—Juvenile literature | Hillary, Edmund, 1919–2008—Juvenile literature | Mountaineering—Everest, Mount (China and Nepal) —Juvenile literature | Everest, Mount (China and Nepal) —Juvenile literature
Classification: LCC GV199.92.T46 H38 2026 (print)
LCC GV199.92.T46 (ebook)
LC record available at https://lccn.loc.gov/2025022984
LC ebook record available at https://lccn.loc.gov/2025022985

Editor: Alyssa Sorenson
Direction and Layout: Molly Ballanger
Illustrator: Cesar Samaniego

Printed in the United States of America at Corporate Graphics in North Mankato, Minnesota.

Table of Contents

On Top of the World

It is March 10, 1953. Tenzing Norgay guides a group of climbers toward Mount Everest.

This mountain is in Asia. At 29,030 feet (8,848 meters), it is the tallest mountain in the world. It is dangerous to climb. People have died trying.

Tenzing is a **Sherpa** climber. He has been to Mount Everest six times. But he has never reached the **summit**. No one has.

The mountain takes weeks to climb. One day, the group sets up camp near a frozen waterfall. It is called the Khumbu Icefall.

Khumbu Icefall

John Hunt is the leader. He picks the best climbers to go to the top. Tenzing is one of them! Tenzing straps **crampons** to his boots. They will help his feet grip ice and snow as he climbs.

Tenzing's climbing partner is Edmund Hillary.
The two men hike up the frozen waterfall.

A rope stretches between them. One day, Edmund falls into a **crevasse**. Tenzing grabs the rope. He pulls Edmund to safety.

It is hard work reaching the summit. As they go higher up the mountain, there is less **oxygen** in the air. It is hard to breathe.

On May 26, Tenzing and Edmund reach 26,000 feet (7,925 m). This area of the mountain is called the Death Zone. They rest in tents at night. They breathe oxygen from tanks to stay alive.

Tenzing and Edmund keep going. They climb to 27,900 feet (8,500 m). A small team helps them set up their last camp. They put the tent on a narrow ledge.

The team says goodbye and heads down the mountain. Tenzing and Edmund are on their own now. They will try to reach the summit tomorrow.

It is 6:30 a.m. on May 29. Tenzing leads the way up a steep **slope**. It is –13 degrees Fahrenheit (–25 degrees Celsius). Tenzing and Edmund are buried up to their hips in snow. It is hard to move.

They reach 28,700 feet (8,750 m) at 9:00 a.m. They are just below the summit. Will they make it?

One more cliff stands in their way. It is 40 feet (12 m) high. There is a small crack in the cliff. It is coated in ice. Tenzing digs his crampons and axe into the ice. He wriggles upward.

Tenzing and Edmund are about 200 feet (61 m) away from the top. They climb one last **ridge**. They see blue sky and clouds.

After five hours of climbing that day, they reach the summit! Tenzing raises his arm in victory. He and Edmund are the first people to reach the top of Mount Everest. They take in the view.

People remember Tenzing and Edmund. They **inspire** mountain climbers everywhere.

Tenzing's Timeline

March 10, 1953
Tenzing's group leaves Kathmandu, Nepal, for Mount Everest.

March 30–April 6, 1953
The group practices climbing in valleys near Mount Everest.

April 12, 1953
The group sets up camp at the foot of Khumbu Icefall.

April 26, 1953
Tenzing saves Edmund from a crevasse.

May 26, 1953
Tenzing and Edmund reach 26,000 feet (7,925 m). They breathe oxygen from tanks to survive.

May 28, 1953
Tenzing and Edmund set up their last camp.

May 29, 1953
Tenzing and Edmund reach the summit of Mount Everest.

Tenzing's Journey

What was Tenzing's path to the top of Mount Everest? Take a look!

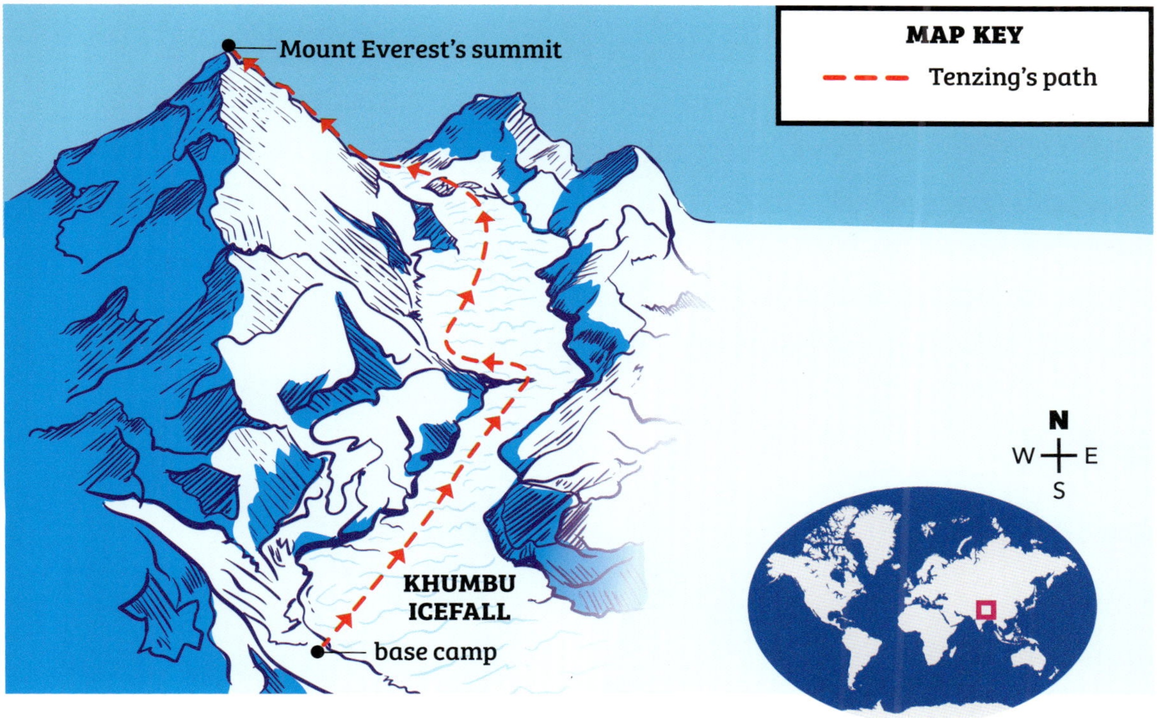

To Learn More

Finding more information is as easy as 1, 2, 3.

1. Go to www.factsurfer.com
2. Enter "**Tenzing Norgay**" into the search box.
3. Choose your book to see a list of websites.

Glossary

crampons: Spiked iron that climbers wear on boots to keep from slipping.

crevasse: A deep crack in ice.

inspire: To influence or encourage someone to do something.

oxygen: A colorless gas found in the air that is needed to breathe.

ridge: A narrow, raised strip on a mountain.

Sherpa: A person who lives in the Himalayas and guides and carries supplies for mountain climbers.

slope: An upward or downward slant of land.

summit: The highest point on a mountain.

Index